A LIMERICK'S ALWAYS A VERSE

200 Original Limericks

A LIMERICK'S ALWAYS A VERSE

200 Original Limericks

Composed, Edited, and Annotated
by **Laurence Perrine**
B.A., M.A., Ph.D., D.H.L., P.D.Q., T.G.I.F. and
Limerick Laureate of northeast Dallas County
(Self-Appointed)

Harcourt Brace Jovanovich, Publishers

San Diego   New York   Chicago   Austin   Washington, D.C.
London   Sydney   Tokyo   Toronto

ISBN: 0-15-551003-7

Library of Congress Catalog Card Number: 89-85709

Printed in the United States of America

According to his powers, each may give;
Only on varied diet can we live.
The pious fable and the dirty story
Share in the total literary glory.

W.H. Auden: Letter to Lord Byron, III

ABOUT THE AUTHOR

Laurence Perrine's textbooks, *Sound and Sense, Story and Structure, Dimensions of Drama*, and *Literature: Structure, Sound, and Sense* have brought millions of college students to appreciate literature. Professor Perrine is Frensley Professor of English, Emeritus, at Southern Methodist University, where he taught from 1946 to 1981.

PREFACE

A limerick is not a form of poetry, it is a form of verse. Much poetry is also written in verse, but poetry soars higher, plunges deeper, and sails in wider circles. Poetry does things that limericks cannot do—express grief and ecstasy, love and hate. It vividly depicts the grandeur and squalor of our planet; it sends probes into outer space; it brings back reports from the interior of the human heart. A limerick, conversely, is primarily designed to elicit laughter. Its central virtue is to be clever. When it attempts to be much more than that, it does so at its peril.

It is not its brevity that keeps the limerick from achieving the higher realms of poetry. Tennyson needs only six lines to depict awesome power and majesty in "The Eagle." The anonymous author of "Western Wind" requires only four to evoke a cry of such passionate yearning that it resonates with undiminished force after five hundred years. Robert Frost captures the essence of a lifetime, animal or human, in his two-liner, "The Span of Life." What chiefly prevents the limerick from such achievements is not its overall brevity, but the brevity of its lines, the quickness of its meter, and the close proximity and consequent insistence of its rhymes.

Strictly defined, the limerick is a verse form consisting of five lines: the first, second, and fifth having three metrical feet (or "beats") and rhyming together; the third and fourth lines having two metrical feet and rhyming together; the meter is prevailingly anapestic, but considerable variation is allowed in the initial foot of each line. In anapestic meter the basic rhythmical unit (or "foot") has two unaccented syllables followed by one accented syllable (ta-da-DAH). Because the anapestic foot has twice as many unaccented as accented syllables, it tends to be swifter—more light on its feet—than the iambic (ta-DAH). The writer can lighten it still further by the use of disyllabic or trisyllabic rhymes, which in addition to adding more unaccented syllables to the lines without increasing the number of feet, also afford the writer opportunity for a virtuosic display of ingenuity in rhyming. Thus, the very qualities that keep the limerick from entering the higher realms of poetry make it a superb form for accomplishing the lesser tasks of literature—for sweeping up the crumbs, as it were, after the banquet.

Like the folk ballads of the Middle Ages, limericks are a *popular* literature. They are spread chiefly by the spoken rather than by the printed word. In this process of oral transmission the names of the original authors are forgotten, and the lines themselves get changed, for better or worse, from recitation to recitation. The anthologist who collects them in print must usually accredit them to *Anon.* or *Unknown*, and must often choose from several versions that have come down to him or her. A signed book—such as the one you hold in your hand at present—paradoxically attempts both to defeat and to further that process. It endeavors to preserve the original design and to give proper credit to its author. But the better the limericks are, the more likely they are to be recited widely, inaccurately, and anonymously. Thus, the limerick writer ambivalently wants both to be remembered and to be forgotten.

The limerick is unlimited in subject matter, but sharply limited in what it can do with that subject matter. Typically, the content of limericks ranges from nonsensical to satirical, from innocent to bawdy. The limericks of Edward Lear, godfather of the limerick, were written for children during the era of Victorian prudery, and are "pure nonsense"; that is, both purely nonsensical and impeccably chaste—completely free of sexual content or allusion.*

It is ironic that the form made famous by the innocent Lear should so quickly become identified, in the minds of many, exclusively with bawdry. But, of course, the limerick is excellently suited for the humorous treatment

---

*Edward Lear neither invented nor named the limerick form. He borrowed the form (and acknowledged the debt) from two obscure pamphlets published by an anonymous author in the early 1820s: *Anecdotes and Adventures of Fifteen Gentlemen* and *History of Sixteen Wonderful Old Women*. Lear's importance is that the immense popularity of his *Book of Nonsense* (1846) and *More Nonsense* (1877), containing between them 212 limericks, each accompanied by a pen-and-ink illustration, established a vogue for the limerick that peaked perhaps in the second decade of the present century but shows no signs of dying in the next-to-last (1989). Lear charmed Victorian readers by the absurdity of his verses and the matching absurdity of his drawings. How much appeal the verses would have had without the drawings is a matter for speculation. Lear paradoxically did not know that he was writing limericks (he called them "nonsense verses"), for the term had almost certainly not yet come into the language. Its earliest recorded use in the *OED* is dated 1896. How, when, and why Lear's form came to be called *limerick* is still a mystery.

of all subjects, and sex, so central in our lives, offers an almost infinite variety of phenomena suitable for comic treatment. It is regrettable that the two chief genres into which limericks are usually classified are the printable and the unprintable, but it may be useful to make a distinction between those designed merely to elicit laughter at aspects of the human condition and those which wish to shock or titillate by the sensationalism of their materials (e.g., the countless limericks relating the outrageous sexual behavior of a pope with one or more nuns).

Though the limerick is still defined in some dictionaries as a form of nonsense verse, few limericks by later authors are as nonsensical as Lear's, and limericks need not be nonsensical at all. The main burden placed on the limerick is that it be witty, ingenious, clever—not that it be nonsensical. Lear's limericks are nonsensical by being virtually pointless. His final line is typically a near replica of his opening line, thus robbing the limerick of any point. For the modern limerick writer the last line is the grand climax to which the first four lead up. It must be either a kicker or a clincher, a surprise or a confirmation. The limerick may have a serious purpose so long as its treatment is comic.

Though I tried, at the beginning of this discussion, to draw a sharp line between the limerick and poetry, it is ultimately impossible to do so. The limerick perhaps most nearly trespasses on poetic territory when it is satirical, for satire is often drawn from those deeper wells of feeling and indignation that also give rise to poetry. Jonathan Swift could have written excellent limericks if he had been acquainted with the form.

In this book I have been open to all of its kinds—the nice, the naughty, the nonsensical, and the satirical. If I may praise my own book for any merit, I claim for it the virtue of variety. My extravagant hope is that there may be found in it two or three limericks that the reader will not choose or be able to forget.

L.P., July 1989

CONTENTS

A LIMERICK'S ALWAYS A VERSE

200 Original Limericks

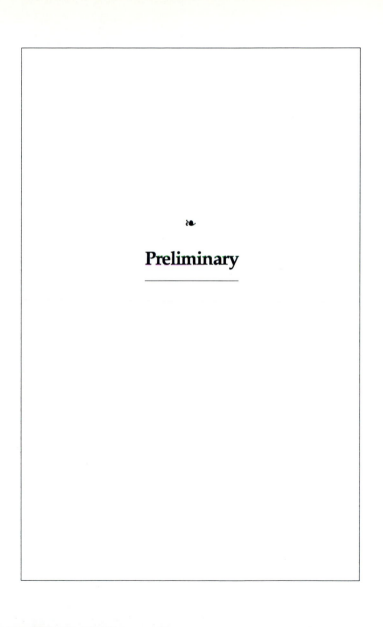

છે

Preliminary

1

The limerick's never averse
To expressing itself in a terse
    Economical style,
    And yet, all the while,
The limerick's *always* a verse.

❧

2

CAVEAT EMPTOR

I have to confess for it's true,
That some of these verses are blue.
    If blue makes you blush
    Like a blooming rose bush
You may join in the cry at that hue.

▪

Academic Exercises

3

RECESSIONAL

A procession of young Ph.D's
Was attacked by a column of bees.
    With B.A's and M.A's
    They fled in a daze
And only crept back by degrees.

❦

4

When he'd read to the end of his lecture
On pre-Byzantine architecture,
   He found his class deep
   In post-Byzantine sleep
For reasons he couldn't conjecture.

૎

5

There was a professor of botany
Whom his students called Dr. Monotony.
    He'd talk on for hours
    On the sex lives of flowers.
Of his own, they alleged, he'd not got any.

⁂

6

Our dean, a disciple of Socrates
And master of many philosophies,
    Because of "brain drain"
    Suffers headaches and strain.
He fears he is losing his faculties.

❧

7

A medical student named Jones
Learned all about all of the bones,
    The muscles, the senses,
    The nerves, and the menses,
And the nurses' erogenous zones.

›⚫

≈

The Arts—Fine and Unrefined

8

A resolute painter named Beth
Almost at the moment of death
    With a charred piece of coal
    Tried to capture her soul
But discovered she'd drawn her last breath.

❧

9

An erudite scholar of Mich-
elangelo, Braque, and Van Dyke
    Confessed, "For my part,
    I know all about art,
But I no longer know what I like."

➜

10

A painter, his canvas still wet,
Said, "No, we're not finished as yet.
    When you pose in the nude
    There's a short interlewd
While we wait for the colors to set."

ٮ

11

A painter of *avant-garde* art

Did a "portrait" of young Arthur Hart.

    Hart's widow, they say,

    Cried out in dismay:

"It's a painting—but, sir, is it Art?"

ʈ♨

12

SOVIET REALISM

To the Soviet chiefs I'd impart:
One can't get a head without heart.
    You're learning too late
    That the art of the state
Is seldom the state of the art.

❦

13

A ceramicist shouted, "Great Scott!
I smoke marijuana. Why not?"—
    "Because, in a way,
    You too are clay,
And I hate to see clay go to pot."

      ❧

14

"The secret of art in ballet,"
I once heard a dance master say,
   "Is how not to bump any
   Member of the company
Who happens to leap the wrong way."

❧

15

Our music is technically slack,
Inharmonious, noisy, and black,
    Its ear-splitting strain
    Makes the brain cry, "Refrain!
O Johann Sebastian come Bach!"

❧

16

OVERTURE

I like the conductor. He hums.
And the violoncellist. She strums.
But, oh! the percussion!
That "1812" Russian!
Must he settle old scores on *my* drums?

&

17

Violin virtuoso renowned,
Smith gave as his reason when found
    In amorous strife
    With his manager's wife
"Oh, I just like to fiddle around."

❦

18

COMPOSURE

Though eighty, I keep on composing—
Yes, even while dining or dozing—
    For, after I'm dead,
    In the decades ahead,
I'll spend all my time de-composing.

⁎

19

I examined TV. For a fact,
It's with sex and with violence packed.
    It drains one of hope
    That with acres of "soap"
It cannot clean up its own act.

▪

20

MANY-STORIED MANHATTAN

It isn't without trepidation
That I go to New York on vacation,
 Where the buildings, they say,
 Are so tall that they *sway*!
Do these stories have any foundation?

&

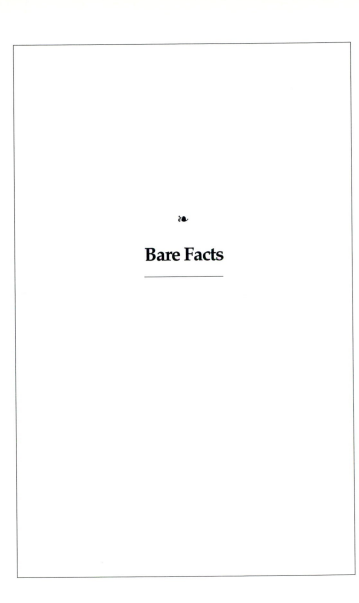

Bare Facts

21

"Will you come to the Animal Fair?
All the birds and the beasts will be there."
   Thus man to his madam.
   Eve answered, "But Adam,
I haven't a thing I can wear."

&

22

A professional dancer, Miss Fairleigh,
Was hauled into court, fair and squarely.
    Asked, "Did you dance lewdly?
    Seductively? Nudely?"
Said, "No, yes, no, well yes, barely."

ॐ

23

The nudists had lain in the sun
Ever since the day's heat had begun.
    Asked a headwaiter there,
     "Do you like your rump rare,
Or would you prefer it well done?"

✿

24

The nudists, by pure thoughts possessed,
Were gathered for prayer before rest,
    But one wanton boy
    Eyed his ravishing Joy
And dreamt how she'd look fully dressed.

↊

25

A budding performer still new to
The art of ballet doffed her tutu
    And danced in the nude.
    It was arty, not lewd,
But in toto the act was still "too . . . too. . . . "

∾

26

In a musical show titled "Hair,"
The performers had nothing to wear.
A novel reversal
Was "undress rehearsal"
Where only the stage wasn't bare.*

&.

*See end note.

&

Courtship and Seduction

27

A grumpy old owl at the zoo,
Hearing other birds' soft bill and coo,
    Hooted, "Silly chit-chit!
    Just *listen* to it!
Thank God, I've more wit than to woo!"

            ❧

28

EXIT NYMPH, CHASED BY APOLLO

Though it was a god who pursued,
Chaste Daphne was "not in the mood."
    Said she, "I shall flee
    Till I'm turned to a tree."
(She would rather be wood than be wooed.)

❦

29

In the spring I am always afraid
For the honor of young man and maid.
    I tremble with dread
    Lest a lad be misled
And I shudder to see one miss laid!

⩊

30

The pretty twins, Lottie and Lou,
I shyly had long wished to woo,
    When, intent to assist me,
    They suddenly kissed me.
I confessed, "I've long wanted you { to."
                                            too."
                                            two."

                    ந

31

My dear Mr. Mortimer Lee,
I respect your "pure passion" for me.
    I honor your chart
    Of the state of your heart—
But why is your hand on my knee?

&.

32

When I offered, shy cousin, unique
Instruction in kissing technique,
    And swore my instruction
    Stopped short of seduction—
I spoke with my tongue in your cheek.

ੲ

33

She was lavish with cuddles and krs.
But denied me the bliss of all blrs:
    "We may cuddle and kiss
    While we're Mr. and Miss—
Nothing more till we're Mr. and Mrs."

&da;

34

Dear Prudence,
    Don't take me in earnest
When I say that my soul's fiery-furnaced
    Yet constant and true,
    For I fear, if you do,
You'll find you're, Miss, taken in.

                            Ernest

              ও

35

COURTING

Two young people, expert at sports,
Played a love game at tennis resorts,
 But when they were wed
 They quarreled instead,
And soon they were back in the courts.

🙙

36

After choir rehearsal the slim
And attractive soprano would skim
    To the dim crypt below
    With the vicar and show
That she kept herself holy for hymn.

⃦

37

Roared her father, severest of men,
"You've lost your virginity then?"
   "I'm sorry, dear father,
   I've been such a bother.
I swear I shan't lose it again."

&

38

THE ROYAL PHYSICIAN STATES HIS POSITION ON HER VIRGIN HIGHNESS'S PRESENT CONDITION

Of that bulge in her waistline I daren't
Proclaim with assurance inerrant
   That she's growing too fat,
   For it's possible that
What she will be will soon be apparent.

                ❧

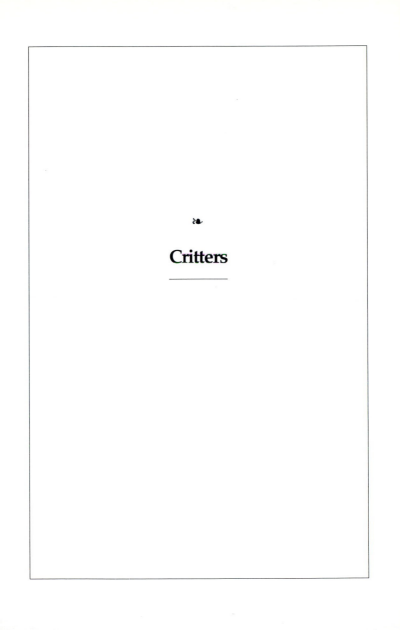

Critters

39

For beauty the swan takes the crown:
On a river where others would drown,
    She floats like a dream
    Eider down or upstream,
And what bears her up is her down.

☙

40

The cuckoo, bird-scholars attest,
Lays her eggs in another bird's nest.
 She's not really crazy,
 Just terribly lazy,
Thinks surrogate motherhood best.

&

41

I've a parrot whose upkeep is steep
But whose knowledge of language is deep.
How richly she scores
On the sparrows outdoors,
Whose small talk is only "cheep cheep!"

❧

42

A monkey sprang down from a tree
And angrily cursed Charles D.
    "I hold with the Bible,"
    He cried. "It's a libel
That man is descended from me!"

ॐ

43

The world's in a terrible shape
Due to man, not gorilla or ape.
    The apes and gorillas
    Are peace-minded fellows:
Don't hoard. Don't murder. Don't rape.

&

44

The cats have their own catechism
To compete with the dogs' dogmatism,
   On part of which logs
    That between cats and dogs
There exists a per-pet-you-all schism.

       ह

45

When our pony caught cold in her breast,
She was boxed in her stall for a rest.
  She complained to the vet,
   "I'm not dying yet—
I'm just a wee hoarse in the chest."

♪

46

The bears face a fate that is terrible,
Foretold in an ancient bear parable,
    How that grim reaper, Man,
    Playing catch-as-catch-can,
Will soon make the bears' state unbearable.

❧

47

WIDOWER

My wife and I strolling one day
In the woods met a bear at his play.
    He was friendly and sunny
    Till I called my wife "Honey."—
Oh, that was the wrong thing to say!

❧

48

The leopard, my guidebook assures,
Can *not* change the spots he abjures.
    But why should he want to?
    There's one thing he *can* do:
He will happily rearrange yours.

❪

49

LEO REX

Two lions, mates, cubs—eight in all—
Fell into a trap, walking tall.
    It was early September,
    I clearly remember,
For the pride had preceded the fall.

ॐ

❧

Deep Thoughts

50

WHOSE REIGN?

No rainfall had watered their plants
Till they did an old Indian dance;
    Then the skies opened wide,
    But they still can't decide,
Was it due to their chants or to chance?

❦

51

A MONK'S ALLEGORY

For each human act there's a place meant:

For looking, the eyes are a casement;

    Conversation Socratic

    Takes place in the Attic;

And sex acts end up in debasement.

ঌ

52

HAVE I A VOICE IN MAKING A CHOICE OR IS IT SOME FORCE DETERMINES MY COURSE?

As I ponder my climb up life's hill,
If you ask me whose will I fulfill,
   As I *must* or I *can*, sir,
   I make you this answer:
I'm *determined* to do what I *will*.

&

53

By prayer or by gifts to the gods
Man has long tried to altar the odds;
    It eternally cheers us
    To think that He hears us
When it often appears that He nods.

*

54

How marred are the lives of the married!

How hard are the lives of the harried!

 I'd endorse suicide,

 Did my wit not deride:

"How bare are the lives of the buried!"

❦

55

Creator, please send us a sign!
Were we shaped by a purpose divine?
    Out of deep melancholy
    We pray, in our folly,
On the *chance* we were made by *design*.

⇢

ಖ

Embarrassments

56

At a party that now they deplore,
The talk was offensive. What's more,
   The parson got loaded,
   The vicar exploded,
But the canon was just a small bore.

57

She carried one egg in her basket.
The moral? You hardly need ask it.
　　She stumbled and broke
　　Both the shell and the yolk:
"Don't put *all* your egg in one basket."

❧

58

The jester rushed in and confessed:
"The man who just died was my guest.
    I had poisoned a cup,
    And he drank it right up,
But I swear all I said was *in jest*!"

૏

59

For years I was humble, till when
I saw myself humblest of men.
    That filled me with pride
    Till I burst, and near died.
Now I'm proud to be humble again.

❧

ào

Family (and Other Foreign) Relations

60

SIBLINGS

We fought over who was the winner
Of a game we called "Who's the Worse Sinner?"
    Till our mother cried, "Well,
    You may both go to hell!
But be sure to be back before dinner."

&

61

When my daughter describes an event
She is sure I will grasp her intent:

"Well, you know what I mean."

Oh, naive seventeen!

I *never* am sure what she meant.

❧

62

I asked, "Do you like Cousin Sue?"
Said Ann, "It's impossible to.
    She's obedient, dutiful,
      Accomplished, and beautiful.
And everyone thinks, 'Why aren't you?'"

❦

63

"Have you any close relatives living?"
My lawyer asked, patiently sieving.
   Said I, "Yes, a gross.
   But they're really *too* close.
They're forbearing but not much for giving."

❧

64

Two families continued a fight

Over which owned a picturesque site

    Until all were bereft.

    Then the only one left

Loudly shouted, "This proves we were right!"

₞

THE MIND DIVIDED AGAINST ITSELF

"I did what I did," declared Id.
"I wish you had hid what you did,"
    Said Ego.   "Amigo,"
    Proclaimed Superego,
"We shouldn't have done what you did."

ॐ

Grave Affairs

_____

66

Twin sisters named Coral and Carol
Were laid out in their finest apparel.
    Their lives had been moral.
    For Carol a chorale
Was sung, and for Coral a carol.

❦

67

They buried the young village whore
In a graveyard not far from the shore.
    She was not distressed
    When they laid her to rest.
She had often been laid there before.

❦

68

My friend on his deathbed lay low.
He'd not let us pity him though.
 He explained with light laughter,
 "What happens hereafter,
I really am dying to know."

&

69

My computer's gone totally dead.
The technicians could see it ahead.
   For a week on its screen
   There were blotches of green.
"It's a terminal illness," they said.

&

70

"To Necropolis, City of Death,"
An ancient philosopher saith,
 "All reluctantly go;
 Yet no matter how slow,
On arrival, we're all out of breath."

    Ș

71

A blossoming virgin named Violet,
Made famous in sonnet and triolet,
    Is here laid to rest
    In violet dressed—
A Violet in violet inviolate.

∾

72

It's *joy* that a funeral needs
To honor man's life and his deeds,
    So we'd heaped on his tomb
    Great masses of bloom,
When his widow arrived wearing weeds.

                                                      ૐ

Historical Hysteria

THE HISTORY OF RELIGION
(One Version)

For deities Greeks had a run;
Jews whittled the list down to one;
Thence arose opportunity
For three-in-one unity.
The Christian community won.*

❧

*But atheists say there are none.

74

"If we let the Greeks in, they'll betray us,"
Helen warned Trojan wives from her dais.
"I fear men'll flay us,
I fear men'll slay us,
But mostly I fear—Menelaus!"

❧

CAESAR AND CLEOPATRA

What word sent he home, mighty Caesar,
To the city of Rome to appease her?
    Not "I came, saw, and conquered"—
    But concordantly structured:
"EYE SEES HER! I, CAESAR! AYE, SEIZE HER!"

              ॐ

76

A Puritan looked at his yard,*
And beckoned his bride to regard—
    "It's no sin to employ it,
    Just sin to enjoy it.
Between us it's awfully hard."

೩

yard = the virile member (17th century). See end note.

77

Marie Antoinette, it is said,

In reports from the land of the dead,

    Suffers torturing ache

    On a diet of cake,

While she yearns for a slice of French bread.

⁎

DARWIN DISCUSSED AT THE BARS
IN THE LONDON ZOO, 1860

"We monkeys look out for each other,"
One monkey remarked to another;
    "No creed hold I deeper
    Than 'I'm brother's keeper,'
But I'm damned if I'm *my* keeper's brother!"

                                             ૐ

79

"Our Congress deserves commendations
For granting the Indian nations
    Great tracts of land free.
    Do you not agree?"—
"Well-l-l, yes, with some large reservations."

☙

80

Two brothers devised what at sight
Seemed a bicycle crossed with a kite.
    They predicted—rash pair!
    It would fly through the air!
And what do you know? They were Wright!

↪

CELEBRITY
(20th Century)

If your features are sexy and glamorous,
And you're healthy, and wealthy, and amorous,
    How unhappy your lot!
    Condemned to be shot
Every day by a battery of cameras.

❦

82

What used to be sternly prohibited,
In these days is freely exhibited,
   A maiden once "pure,"
   "Chaste," "virtuous," sure
Today is called "strongly inhibited."

❦

83

In former days fearless freebooters
Faced us openly with their six-shooters,
    But the ways of their heirs
    Are more subtle than theirs:
They do it all now with computers.

❦

ஒ

Indulgences and Addictions

84

DRUNKARD'S PROGRESS

At first he stood up for a drink.
He sat down for a second I think.
    Then, third, from the floor
    He gave fourth a roar,
Killed a fifth, and was sick under sink.

⁚

85

She confided one day to the Vicar:
"My husband is given to liquor.
 He'll attend Sunday mass
 For a sip from the glass
And a wafer becoming soused quicker."

&❧

THE FORCED FAST CURE

She couldn't resist food a bit.
And fat? She was dying of it.
 She cried, "I'll be bound
 When food is around
You must see I am tied to be fit."

87

Though his mother had said to him, "Never
Eat fast, it's a fatal endeavor,"
    He ate faster and faster
    Till he met with disaster,
And now he is fasting forever.

❧

88

Can anyone living recall
One person with ego so small
    That they've given up smoking
    Without then invoking
Any notice from others *at all*?

⇢

THE STRAIGHT DOPE
(A Review)

The hero of this rather silly
New movie's a lowlife from Chile;
    But the heroin—my!
    She's as high as the sky—
A blueblood Main Liner from Philly.

❖

ße

Literary Musings: Views and Reviews

89

A sure source of steamy sensation,
Of scandal and sin and temptation,
   Was our neighborhood gossip,
   All-knowing Miss Ossip.
We all called her Miss Information.

ﻼ

91

Other poets may write to a Muse
Whom they line up to worship in queues
    With long invocations
    And loud adulations.
My verses are writ to amuse.

❢

92

A passion for rhyme is my curse.
Over time it gets worse and worse.
    All rhyme is my treasure.
    I measure my pleasure
By its number of couplings per verse.

›●

93

Is true verse or free verse the sweeter?
Well, true verse is certainly neater.
    This verse isn't free!
    It is metered, you see—
So put a small fee in the meter.

⁄

94

O Britain! what glories are thine!
The greatest: your language divine;
   The language of Shakespeare,
   Of Keats, Milton (Blake's peer),
And the language of Laurence Perrine!

ℊ

MIDSUMMER NIGHT'S DREAM

Dear Bottom the weaver, alas!
You've been given the head of an ass.
    Long ears, you have gott'em,
    But bear in mind, Bottom,
At bottom you're no horse's ass!

                            ❧

96

THE MOOR OF VENICE

When Othello fell victim to jealousy,
He instantly grew over-zealous. He
    Saw not the offense
    Was his own in a sense—
A fallacy few jealous fellows see.

❦

THE SCARLET LETTER

Although Hester's own pastor possessed her,
The way she faced up to it blessed her.
    When they said, "Mistress Prynne,
    You've committed a sin,"
'Twas a red-letter day for Ms. Hester.

&

98

THE TELEPHONE BOOK
(A Review)

No other author's amassed
So large and so varied a cast,
  But of action or plot
  I cannot find a jot.
Best seller! Not destined to last.

❧

99

I asked my muse out for a date.
She arrived at my trysting place late.
    I was very put out,
    Which explains, without doubt,
Why this limerick has sagged so badly
    under its wait.

                                ❧

❧

Marriage—and Other Miscarriages

100

It started with billing and cooing,
And that led me on to a wooing,
    But when we were wed
    The cooing stopped dead,
And the billing has been my undoing.

↝

101

The sex life her husband dreamed of,
She considered herself far above.
   He craved osculation
   And *then* copulation!—
She wanted to kiss and make love.

&

102

Since she married for riches and rank
She has only her own self to thank
    That now she's a martyr
    To an arrant self-starter
Who's turned in old age to a crank.

∾

103

There's none but himself he can blame
For yielding his girlfriend his name.
    Now he kisses the missus
    But misses the kisses
Of misses whose kisses inflame.

૎

A PERFECT MATCH

Here lies a young woman from Natchez
Whose passion was playing with matches.
   She married a parson
   Addicted to arson.
Now all that remains is their ashes.

&

105

On their honeymoon travels—good lord!
Each learned that the other one snored;
    Both stoutly denied
    Any fault on their side—
In this only were they in accord.

       ہ

106

A FISH TAIL?

Lady Cynthia Parkerhouse Furman
Met and married, off Finland, a merman,
But whether the woman
Bore babes that were human
Or finnish, we've yet to determine.

❧

107

My dear wife, my precious wife Jewel,
Had a face-lift, a hair-do, a do-all.
    Now to men in the city
    She's witty *and* pretty.
She calls it her urban renewal.

❧

108

My cousin, a cashier named Tillie,
Has suitors named Billy and Willy.
    All day at her till
    She ponders God's will—
Will Will fill the bill or will Billy?

                                  ﻙ

109

My husband's a chatterer who
Speaks as freely as rhyme lets him do.
   He's vivacious, loquacious,
   Audacious. Good gracious!
See! now I am doing it too!

❧

110

He was *always* correcting her grammar.
He said, when she said with a yammer,
    "The reindeer are falling,"
    "The rain, dear, *is* falling."
She beat him to death with a hammer.

❧

111

A jealous old husband named Bell
In a temper-fit killed his wife Nell.
    Though strangling his wife
    Would cost him *his* life,
Bell didn't stop wringing his knell.

❦

112

When I have to leave town for out yonder,
I know my love's heart tends to wander,
    So I squander my money
    On gifts for my honey:
It's presents that make the heart fonder.

                      🙢

113

Well, doesn't it strike you as funny?
Whenever she says to me, "Honey"—
    With such a beginning
    So sweet and so winning—
She's wanting to talk about money?

❧

114

The bandit's son took for his bride
An innocent girl. Horrified
    When she learned from her honey
    The source of his money,
"My in-laws are outlaws," she cried.

▪

115

Because of a neighbor named Kissinger
I've let my wife know I'm dismissing her.
    My wife, much besought,
    Had been chaste, so I thought,
Till I caught Mr. Kissinger kissing her.

⁎

116

Lady Candida, woman of rank,
Wed Sir Francis, who managed a bank.
   They lived without pother
    Because to each other
They were always just Candid and Frank.

⦊

&

Money Matters

117

Should you buy a new hat at the hatter's?
Or call on your banker in tatters?
    You may think "Save or Waste"
    But a matter of taste,
But in matters of money, it matters.

ಬಿ

118

"Red ink in sufficient amount
Can ruin a pool or a fount,"
　　Said my boss, looking blue.
　　"Here's a bottle for you.
Don't spill it on any account."

&

119

Losing money is bad, you would think,
But tax write-offs color the ink.
    When his auditor said,
    "This account's in the red,"
Mr. Richman was just tickled pink.

❧

120

FOR AN IRS OFFICER
Born April 15, 19—

Her IRS officer yearns
To take every penny she earns,
    So on Skake-Down-the-Earth Day
    She writes on a birthday
Card, "Many unhappy returns!"

❧

121

There was a young man with an ax
Who rebelled against filing a tax.
    "Just think of the cost
    And the time that is lost!
Next year I shall file my ax."

❢

122

There once was a miser who hoarded,
And a harlot who stripped, and then more did.
    And, you know, it is funny:
    What each did for money,
The other regarded as sordid.

૎

123

A miser, of burglars the prey,
Had half his gold stolen away.
    He spent all that night
    In a terrible fright
And he spent all the rest the next day.

❦

124

She's so rich that her pockets go "Chink!"
But she's not so well off as you think.
    In an ill-starred *amour*
    With her private chauffeur
She was literally driven to drink.

ಎ

125

He found he could not pay his rent.
His paycheck was all of it spent.
    He's agreed to engage
    At the then-going wage,
And like all going wages—it went!

•

126

"I'm broke," cried the youth at a smoker,
"I've lost all I have, playing poker."
    "You joke," said a friend,
    "Though you think this the end,
I'm sure I can find you a broker."

&.

127

An honest lad, he was unwilling
To sell off his soul for a shilling,
    So, not one to shirk,
    He did ten years' hard work;
Then he sold it for ninety pounds sterling.

❧

128

CHANGE

To all who for fortune have burned
Or at least for stability yearned,
   Remember the times:
   Spend your nickels and dimes,
And recite: "Dollar saved, penny earned."

                                                  ዺ

129

What flaw in your make-up and mine
When we go out to shop and to dine
    Makes an item appear
    At $4 too dear
But a bargain at 3.99?

❧

130

Our senators say they begrudge it.
Our congressmen try sometimes to nudge it.
    But our national debt
    Grows heavier yet,
And nobody up there can budget.

૎

131

COMMUNIST

That prized Grecian urn was so rare—
The possession of one millionaire—
    That, evading the guards,
    He reduced it to shards,
So that everyone there got a share.

❧

132

CAPITALIST

He asserts that the laissez faire creed
Is a capital theory indeed.
    It makes people itch
    To produce and get rich,
Though its warrant's not need, it's agreed.

❧

ა

Politics and Power

133

Though his "virtues" as king were unneeded,
None ever tried harder than he did
    To become one. With others
    He killed ten elder brothers
And then—well, of course, he succeeded.

›♠‹

134

ON THE LAST ELECTION

Political office, alas,
Goes often to men who are crass.
   Was Caligula coarse
   In appointing a horse?
Look! We have elected an ass!

❖

135

Campaigners for office are cunning,
Their feats on their feet often stunning.
    They can take a firm stand
    (On sufficient demand)
And even can lie while they're running.

❀

136

THE POPULAR WILL

On the campaign trail, one supposes,
Will eagerly counts eyes and noses.
   When elected, Will knows,
   He will count Aye's and No's
That might kill any bill Will proposes.

❦

137

A delegate wearing a banner
Behaved with a hostess, Miss Tanner,
    At a party convention,
    I'm sorry to mention,
In a most unconventional manner.

₮

138

CONVENTION DAZE

No easy committee was ours.

We sat, we debated our powers.

 Each motion, each second,

 Our chairwoman reckoned,

From reading the minutes, took hours.

ઢ

139

U.N. DELEGATE

He thought long and hard how he'd greet
The new foreign friends that he'd meet:
    "I'm a German." "I'm Syrian."
    "I'm a Cuban." "I'm Algerian."
Should he sigh, "I'm a . . . No! I'm from Crete."

❧

140

BICENTENNIAL

Born after a fierce revolution,
Now a two-centuries old institution,
My Uncle Sam's health
Rests not on his wealth,
But on having a strong constitution.

ᨗ

141

If you kill only one, you're a zero,
A murderer baser than Nero;
    But if, in a war,
    You kill eighty score,
By god! you're a national hero!

❦

142

Two nations engaged in a race
To see which could dominate space,
    Till one with aplomb
    Detonated a bomb,
And that put an end to the race.

❦

143

SPLIT SECOND THOUGHTS

When the Russians mailed US an Epistle
That flew through the air with a whistle,
    We waited in doubt
    And suspense to find out
Was it missive or missal or missile?—
Was it miss-all or instant dismissal?

❦

The Professions— and Their Indiscretions

144

"Be precise from the very first slice,"
Said a surgeon when asked for advice.
  "To the patient below
  It's no comfort to know
That you won't make the same mistake twice."

❧

145

A poet with M.D. diploma
Liked words with a pleasant aroma.
    When pressed for an answer,
    He never said, "Cancer!"
But instead, "You've a cute carcinoma."

∾

146

To be patient no patient's inclined.

They want to know what doctors find,

    And not have to wait

    For the obits to state

The fate to which now they're consigned.

❖

147

PROFESSIONAL SERVICES

He examined with exquisite skill
A call girl who'd suffered a chill,
    Both downside and skinside,
    Both outside and inside—
Then each sent the other a bill.

148

The physicians attendant on Beth
Disputed the cause of her death.
   Agreement was none.
   "Heart failure!" cried one,
And the other, "Cessation of breath!"

        ૎

149

PSYCHIATRIST

She hadn't on even a snip
Between her tight dress and her hip.
  She said, "I forgot."
  He said, "You did not.
You are wearing a Freudian slip."

❧

150

I was rational once—a bit lazy;
Now my mind is all muddled and hazy,
    For last month I kissed
    My psychiatrist,
And now he is driving me crazy.

❦

151

A lawyer is one who would trim
From the language all words that are slim;
    He will always prefer
    To "he died after her"
To aver that "she pre-deceased him."

152

"This case was a good one for me,"
Said a lawyer, collecting his fee.
　　"The victim got stung,
　　The jury was hung,
And the criminal got off scot-free."

ક

153

The bartender said, "It's Judge Carr.
He holds court here daily. So far,
    In this, his oasis,
    He's tried three hundred cases
Since first he was called to the bar."

               ❧

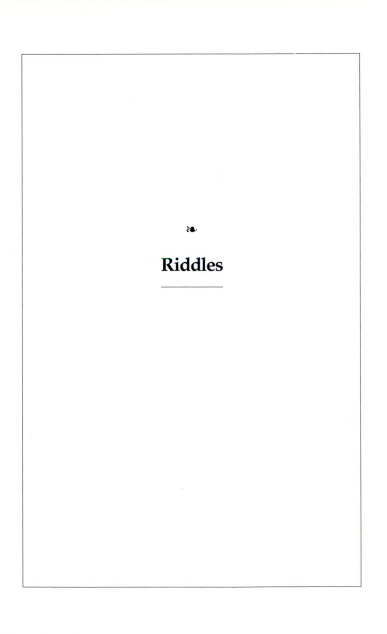

Riddles

154

A limrick's writtn to plas,
Lik a man on a flying trapz.
    I rgrt that this sampl
    Sts no good xampl,
But you may rdm it with as.

›●

155

I have thirteen accountable feet!
Though I sometimes am naughty, I'm neat.
    I'm constructed on lines
    That my species defines,
And I end with a trick that's a treat.

❦

156

Adored by all pre-adolescents,
And a saint to both princes and peasants,
    So abundantly gifted
    Our souls are uplifted,
Not so much by his gifts as his presence.

        ❧

157

He has horns and a crook'd fingernail
And hooves like a goat's. He is male.
    His slippery skin
    Is as scarlet as sin.
Do I need to add further detail?

∾

ᐍ

The Sacred and the Profane

158

A newcomer greeted a saint:
"It's ol' Peter, goddam if it ain't!"
    "Sir, here you may use
    Any language you choose,
But, God damn it! you cannot say 'ain't!'"

&

159

A monk who'd run in to a door
Voiced some very choice oaths from the floor.
    Overheard by another,
    He arose and said, "Brother,
I swear I won't swear any more."

❦

160

EXODUS 34:6-7

Have you never considered it odd
That a self-declared merciful God
    Should punish a grandkid
    For something his gramp did?
It's proclaimed in the Bible, *by God*!

&ra;

161

THE MODEL

Of the crimes for which man is accursed,
Genocide I consider the worst.
 But remember when God
 Sent a forty-day flood?
Though men do it, God did it first.

≥.

162

God wanted mankind to amend,
So he caused a huge flood to descend,
    But, in forty years, men
    Were bad once again—
So much for the means and the end!

                                     🙰

163

God sent us a rainbow back then
As a pledge He'd not do it again.
 Then isn't it odd
 That the phrase "acts of God"
Still appears in the contracts of men?

❦

164

Our God, some contend, is immutable,
And their faith is, indeed, irrefutable:
    When He does what He should,
     It's because "He is good,"
When He doesn't, "His ways are inscrutable."

❦

165

We've been given the Word by our Lord.
It will bring the whole earth to accord.
    His message "Make Peace"
    Gives life a new lease.
We shall spread it by fire and sword.

            ↊

166

THE IDEAL COMMITTEE

When the Trinity goes into session
For judgment, debate, or decision,
   They merge into one
   So their judgments are done
With singular speed and precision.

❧

167

Resurrection!—new body, new face,
My awkwardness turned into grace!
    But God, saint, or elf,
    Will I still be myself?—
Or somebody else in my place?

❦

168

Sighed the Devil seductively, "So!
Let me show you my realm down below,"
    But the more he insisted,
    The more she resisted.
Said she, "I'll be damned if I go!"

❧

169

There was a young fellow from Dallas
Who lived in a Highland Park palace.
  He ate, so I'm told,
  Off a platter of gold,
And drank, so he thought, from a chalice.

❧

170

On one point, and one point alone,
Concerning the known and unknown,
  All religions agree:
  "All creeds that may be
Are in error excepting our own."

ॐ

Sexual Versions (di-, per-, and a-)

171

If the race wasn't lost from the start,
Thus preventing affairs of the heart,
    The cause, I suspect, is
    That *homo erectus*
Found a good place for playing his part.

▶

172

A knowing young couple, the Pecks,
Thought they knew all there was about sex.
    It was just a condition
    Of taking position
And fitting concave to convex.

❦

173

An innocent couple, perplexed,
Asked, "Now that we're married, what next?"
    Lent a book by clinicians
    Called *Sixty Positions*,
They decided, "It's all too complex!"

            ꝫ

174

For a dance date my big sister may
Press her dress, dress her hair a whole day,
    Yet return badly fussed
    If her hair isn't mussed
And her dress in a wild disarray.

૎

175

Some people count sheep, using numbers
To hasten and lengthen their slumbers.
    My nostrum entails
    Counting curvaceous girls,
For I much prefer figures to numbers.

❦

176

If you ask me his future I'd say
With women he'll go a long way.
    He's a keen zest for living,
    A nature for giving,
And a talent for work and foreplay.

❦

Sports—Outdoor and Indoor

177

I once asked a jockey, "Please say,

Does the rider or horse earn the pay?

    Is it you?" His reply

    Was an immodest "Aye!"

His horse only glared and said "Nay-y-y-y!"*

❦

*See end note.

178

Said a sailor who'd never been beat
At sprinting (he'd win by two feet):
    "If I cannot claim place
    As the best in the race,
At least I'm the first of the fleet."

❢

DISSENSION IN THE CLUBHOUSE

From his golf bag there issued a mutter,
Then a gasp was choked out with a sputter.
   He'd been *one* on the green
   But holed out at *sixteen*,
And his driver was strangling his putter.

❦

180

On this, Mr. Duff took his stand,
He would *never* say, "Ain't Nature grand!"
    For his slices and hooks
    Always landed in brooks,
In lakes, or in woods, or in sand.

❦

181

I played chess with my robot at ten,
And he rapidly took all my men.
    When I played him at two
    I'd adjusted a screw,
And now *I'm* the master again.

❧

ಕ

Timely Warnings

182

A clock with but hands and a face
Can run a considerable race,
But a four-legged table
With wings is unable
To stir, and must stay in its place.

&

183

Growing older each year, Mr. Weems
Tries to act just as young as his dreams,
    But his eye for appearances
    Sees his endurance is
Falling apart at the seems.

૎

184

The illusions of youth nearly dead,
I look up and see overhead
    All the golden clouds shining
    To silver declining
And each with a lining of lead!

❦

185

THE SON AND THE PRODIGAL FATHER

"You come to me hoping to borrow
For trollops to lighten your sorrow
　　When you're ninety years old!"—
　　"Now, Sonny, don't scold,
I won't be that old till tomorrow."

&

186

There was an old fellow named Fred.
At his age he should have been dead.
　　But by frequent coition
　　He kept in condition—
Though he seldom stayed long out of bed.

ও

ଔ

Workers and Shirkers

187

GARMENT WORKERS OF AMERICA
Local 47

When engaging in labor disputes,
We called on our cutest recruits.
    Their method was striking
    And quite to my liking
They sued in their old union suits.

∾

188

"I enjoy riding logs to the mill,"
Said an old lumberjack. "Always will.
　　Though one year a tree,
　　Falling, shattered my knee,
You can see that I'm lumbering still."

❧

189

A collector of clocks, Mr. Reiking,
Had a wife very much to my liking.
    "I'll come again soon,"
    I informed him one noon;
"Everything that you have here is striking."

હ•

190

IN HOSPITAL

With what patient and loving good will
Do the aides all their duties fulfill!
    They awake you from sleep,
    No matter how deep,
To take your prescribed sleeping pill.

        ⅈ

191

In head-hunting circles, I've read,
Competition is deeply inbred;
    Their circles are vicious,
    Their wishes pernicious,
All ambitious for getting ahead.

↪

192

IRS AGENT

Whether daylight was waning or waxing,
He never had time for relaxing.
    As income inspector
    And payments collector
He found his work terribly taxing.

⇢

193

I farm alone now, and I ache!
My heart and my back want to break!
    I work down each row
    With a spade and a hoe
Since my wife ran away with a rake.

▪

194

A movie-house owner named Mills
Made corn liquor back in the hills.
    He supported large cars
     Selling moonshine and stars,
Banking income from movies and stills.

                    ❧

195

There once was a forger who said,
"Counterfeiting's my meat and my bread.
　　Now with Feds on my trail,
　　Should I therefore trim sail?
My motto is still 'Forge ahead!'"

❧

196

A ship's captain, dining in state,

At telling sea stories was great.

    He'd a fleet of one-liners

    That shipwrecked the diners

And his wife, whom he called his "first mate."

⁕

197

A baker none thought would succeed
Made a roll that was flavored with mead.
    It was such a success
    That he told IRS,
"I'm making more dough than I knead."

❦

198

A real estate dealer named Potts
Subdivided a desert in plots.
    When asked what he planned
    To sell on this land
With nothing but sand, he said "Lots!"

❦

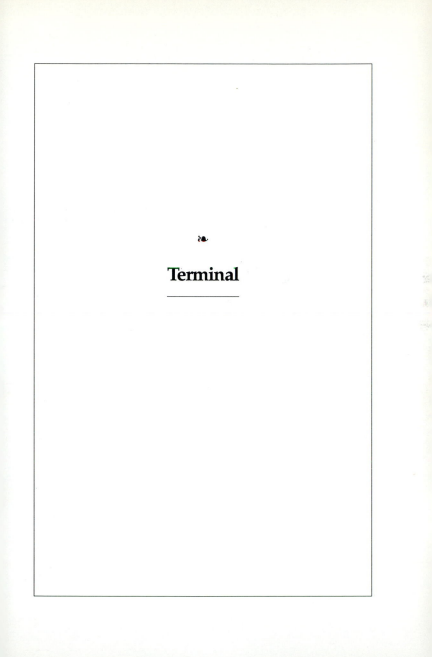

Terminal

199

The name is *Per-RINE*, as you see
(Long *i* and mute terminal *e*);
　　It rhymes with *design*
　　And with *fine* and *divine*!
With *Laurence* (spelled *u*) it is me.

❧

200

IN THE SAME VAIN

May my blessings rest lightly upon
Those who joy in these after I'm gone.
    But curse those who edit
    Assigning for credit
Those imposters *Unknown* and *Anon*.

∾

NOTES

26   The musical comedy "Hair," based on conflict between "the establishment" and the "hippie" counterculture, was produced in New York City in 1967. The first act ends with the entire cast, nude, joining hands and facing the audience to sing the final number.

78   The word yard, in the sense made use of here, is listed in unabridged dictionaries as archaic or obsolete, but it was current in the Puritan era. Shakespeare uses the term in this sense in at least three of his plays, always in a punning context. More recently Robert Graves has revived the term in his poem "Ogres and Pygmies."

117   One jockey, Johnny Langden, won more than 5000 races; another, Eddie Arcaro, won 4779 races. On the other hand, the horse Man o' War won 20 of the 21 races he ran in. The question raised in this limerick is a very real one. Should we bet on the jockey or the horse?

ACKNOWLEDGMENTS

A number of these limericks have been initially published elsewhere: 101 in *Poetry* (Chicago); 1, 66, in *Lettres from Limerick* (now defunct); 9, 22, 29, 30, 37, 39, 42, 74, 80, 100, 154, 158 in annual issues of *Light Year* (Cleveland: Bits Press); 143 in *The Inkling* (Alexandria, MN); 67, 79, 134, 152 in *The Haven: New Poetry* (Albuquerque); 50, 78, 160, 161, 162, 164 in various issues of the *Secular Humanist Bulletin* (Buffalo); and 151 in *The Texas Bar Journal* (Austin). In addition, more than I can mention have first appeared in the monthly newsletter of the Limerick Special Interest Group of *Mensa*.